From Trash to Treasures

Old Clothes

Daniel Nunn

Heinemann Library
Chicago, Illinois

www.heinemannraintree.com
Visit our website to find out more information about Heinemann-Raintree books.

To order:
☎ Phone 888-454-2279
⌨ Visit www.heinemannraintree.com to browse our catalog and order online.

Edited by Rebecca Rissman, Daniel Nunn, and Sian Smith
Designed by Joanna Hinton-Malivoire
Picture research by Tracy Cummins
Originated by Capstone Global Library Ltd
Printed and bound in China by South China Printing Company Ltd

15 14 13 12 11
10 9 8 7 6 5 4 3 2 1

Library of Congress Cataloging-in-Publication Data
Nunn, Daniel.
  Old clothes / Daniel Nunn.
    p. cm.—(From trash to treasures)
  Includes bibliographical references and index.
  ISBN 978-1-4329-5149-8 (hc)—ISBN 978-1-4329-5158-0 (pb) 1. Clothing and dress—Environmental aspects—Juvenile literature. I. Title.
  GT518.N86 2012
  391—dc22   2010049818

Acknowledgments
We would like to thank the following for permission to reproduce photographs: Heinemann Raintree pp. 6, 9, 10, 11, 12, 13, 14, 15, 16, 17, 18, 19, 20, 21, 23a, 23b (Karon Dubke); istockphoto pp. 4b (© Silke Dietze), 7 (© Serhiy Zavalnyuk), 8a (© Craig Veltri), 8b (© WendellandCarolyn), 22a (© Pamela Moore), 22b (© drflet), 22c (© Kseniya Ragozina), 23c (© Craig Veltri); Shutterstock pp. 4a (© stormur), 5 (© Karina Bakalyan), 23c (© homydesign), 23d (© stormur).

Cover photograph of a sock monkey, a sock puppet, and socks and back cover photographs of a bag and a sock puppet reproduced with permission of Heinemann Raintree (Karon Dubke).

Every effort has been made to contact copyright holders of material reproduced in this book. Any omissions will be rectified in subsequent printings if notice is given to the publisher.

Contents

Some words are shown in bold, **like this**. You can find them in the glossary on page 23.

What Are Old Clothes?

 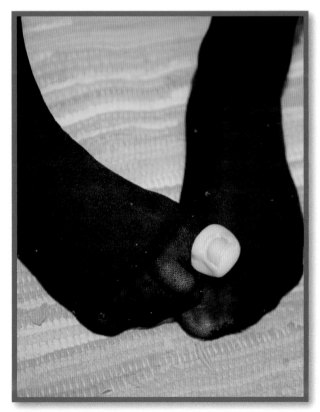

Old clothes are clothes that you don't need anymore.

They might have holes in them, or you might just have grown out of them.

Old clothes can be made of different **materials**.

These sweaters are made of wool.

What Happens When You Throw Old Clothes Away?

Everybody needs clothes.

But when you have finished with them, do you throw them away?

When you throw clothes away, they end up at a garbage dump.

They will be buried in the ground and may stay there for a very long time.

What Is Recycling?

Old clothes can be **recycled** if you put them in a clothing donation box.

When something is recycled, it is broken down and used to make something new.

Clothes that you no longer want can also be given to a **charity** store.

Charities can sell your old clothes or give them to people who need them.

How Can I Reuse Old Clothes?

You can also use old clothes to make your own new things.

When you have finished with an item of clothing, put it somewhere safe.

Soon you will have lots of old clothes waiting to be reused.

You are ready to turn your trash into treasures!

What Can I Make with Old Tights?

You can use old tights to make a snake.

You can fill the inside of your snake with old clothes, too!

rolled-up tights

This flying disk has also been made of old tights.

You can throw it like a Frisbee.

What Can I Make with Old T-Shirts?

Old T-shirts can be really useful.

This T-shirt has been made into a bag.

Old T-shirts can even be made into jewelry!

This girl's necklace and bracelets have been made from an old T-shirt.

What Can I Make with Old Pants?

This bag is made out of a pair of old jeans!

It is a great way to reuse old pants with a hole in the knee.

You can also turn an old pant leg into a **draft guard**.

This can help keep your bedroom warm on a windy winter day.

Make Your Own Sock Puppet

It is easy to make a fun puppet out of an old sock.

You will need a large sock, **felt**, googly eyes, yarn or string, scissors, and glue.

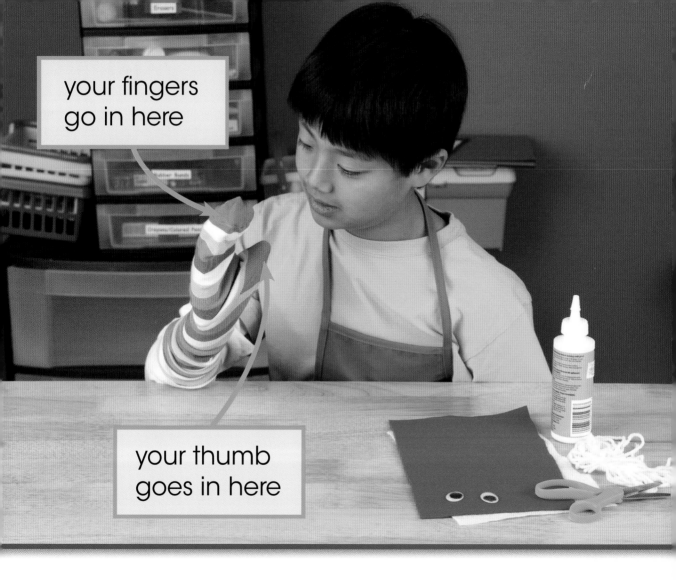

First, pull the sock over your hand.

Your fingers will be the puppet's head, and your thumb will be the puppet's mouth.

Cut a tongue out of red **felt**.

If you do not have any googly eyes, you can make these out of black and white felt.

Glue the eyes, the yarn or string, and
the tongue onto your puppet's head.

Your puppet is finished!

Recycling Quiz

One of these items is made from **recycled** clothes. Can you guess which one? (The answer is on page 24.)

Glossary

 **charity** organization that raises money to help people or animals in need

 **draft guard** long, thin cushion placed along the bottom of a door to stop wind from blowing into a room

 **felt** type of cloth, often used in crafts

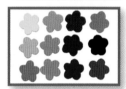 **material** what something is made of

 **recycle** break down a material and use it again to make something new

Find Out More

Ask an adult to help you make fun things with old clothes using the Websites below.

Flying disk: **www.makingfriends.com/recycle/ recycled_tights_frisbee.htm**

Bag: **www.craftsforkids.com/projects/ 1100/1108/1108_4.htm**

Snake: **www.freekidscrafts.com/sleepy_snake_from_ pantyhose-e95.html**

Find other ideas at: **www.freekidscrafts.com/recycled_ clothes_crafts_for_kids_|_recycled_crafts-t72.html**

Answer to question on page 22
The bag is made from recycled clothes.

Index